THE SILLIEST CHRISTMAS JOKE BOOK

FOR KIDS AND FAMILY

RIDDLELAND

TABLE OF CONTENTS

INTRODUCTION

A Message from Santa Claus

Ho ho ho! Merry Christmas, my dear friend. Can you feel it? The air is crisp, the snow glitters like sugar, and the smell of cookies drifts through every cozy home. That can only mean one thing—Christmas is drawing near!

All across the world, children are hanging stockings, wrapping gifts, and decorating their trees with twinkling lights. The carols are playing, the cocoa is warm, and laughter fills the air. But tell me—have you practiced your Christmas jokes yet?

If not, you're in for a treat! Inside this book are over 300 merry jokes—silly puns, playful riddles, and cheerful knock-knock jokes that can make even me laugh until my belly shakes like a bowl full of jelly!

Each chapter is a little Gift from my workshop—Gift One, Gift Two, and Gift Three—each filled with giggles about elves, snowmen, reindeer, and maybe even yours truly. The jokes are neatly organized, so if you ever need a snowman pun for Frosty or a reindeer riddle for Rudolph, you'll find it faster than my sleigh on Christmas Eve.

Some of these jokes have been passed down through generations, told by glowing fireplaces and shared around dinner tables. This book gathers that joyful tradition into one place—so you can keep the laughter alive with your family and friends.

So, pour yourself a mug of cocoa, snuggle under a warm blanket, and turn these pages with the people you love. May this book fill your home with laughter, joy, and the bright sparkle of Christmas spirit.

Ho ho ho! Merry Christmas to you and yours—and remember, the best gift of all is a good laugh shared together.

With love and cheer,
Santa Claus

GIFT ONE:

QUESTION -AND- ANSWER /PUNNY JOKES

Ho ho ho! You've made it to your very first gift. I wrapped this one myself, with a little help from the elves. Inside are some of my favorite jokes—quick puns and clever questions that will make your cheeks jingle with laughter.

Before you open it, here's a secret from the North Pole. Laughter is real Christmas magic. It can warm a room faster than a roaring fire and turn a quiet night into a merry memory. That's why I always add a touch of humor to the season.

These question-and-answer jokes will make you think one thing and laugh when you hear the twist. They're lighthearted, playful, and just a little sneaky, like the elves after too much peppermint fudge.

So pour a cup of cocoa, gather everyone close, and get ready to giggle. Your first gift is waiting. Let the laughter begin!

ADVENT CALENDARS

(For those who have never seen one, an advent calendar is a countdown calendar that counts down the days of December until Christmas Day. Each day typically has a door that opens, revealing a surprise behind it.)

 What has a picture of Santa on it and strains noodles?

An advent colander.

What became of the thief who stole the advent calendar?

He got twenty-five days.

Why did the little boy start to drool on the advent calendar?

His mom said there were going to be four sundaes on his calendar.

Why are the last six calendar days of December considered routine?

They are unadventful.

6

Why did the boy store his advent calendar in the refrigerator?

He wanted the days leading up to Christmas to be cool.

BELLS

 Why is it difficult to hold a conversation
when bells are around?

They always want to chime in.

How do you know
if a bell finds a joke to be funny?

You'll hear peals of laughter.

What name do bells find insulting?

Don't call them "ding-dongs."

What did the bell say when it wanted to change its daily
routine and do something crazy?

"I feel a little dingy today."

What did the bell say
when it had to repeat itself for a third time?

"I tolled you once; I tolled you twice; . . . .

What kind of car does a bell drive?

One with a ding in it.

Who speaks on behalf of all bells?

The ring leader.

How are bells like appreciative audiences?

They have clappers.

How are the bells that chime
the E-note like a stomach?

One is a Bell E and the other is a belly.

What happened to the bell's paycheck?

It got dinged.

Was the bell in favor of
decorating the Christmas tree?

Yes, he gave the idea a ringing endorsement.

What did the female Christmas chime
want to be known as?

A jingle belle.

Before becoming one of the jingle bells,
what job did the bell hold at the circus?

He was the ringmaster.

What kind of bell doesn't make music?

A dumbbell.

Do you know
the holiday pepper recipe?

Ginger, bell, ginger, bell . . .

CANDY CANES

Why was the striped candy cane
so good at hide-and-seek?

It wasn't spotted.

What gift never arrives damaged?

Candy canes are always in mint condition.

Why did the candy cane
go to the doctor?

It felt sucky.

What did the candy cane
say to its girlfriend?

"You're so sweet."

Did you know the original candy cane
was intentionally given a peppermint flavor?

It was mint to be.

How is a strong wind
like a rushing Christmas candy?

Both are "hurry canes."

Why is it important to know that candy canes
were originally designed to look like a shepherd's staff?

It's important to ewe.

Which Christmas candy changes flavors?

The candy cane; it begins as a peppermint, but after you suck it, it becomes pointed, making it a spear mint candy.

Why did the girl place
a candy cane under her pillow?

She hoped to have sweet dreams.

What was the candy cane
boxing champion best known for?

Its hook.

Why was the candy cane
so respected?

It had earned its stripes.

Why does Santa prefer to
land on roofs that slant?

They are in peak condition.

How are a roof and Santa alike?

Kids look up to both.

Why did the roof
go to the doctor's office?

It had shingles.

Why did the chimney
go to the doctor's office?

It had the flu.

What does a roof have
in common with a big river?

Rafters.

Do most people understand
how Santa lands on roofs?

No, roofs are over their heads.

Why do roofers spend so much time talking
about roofs and only roofs?

They are shingle-minded.

Does Santa like beautiful chimneys?

No. He especially despises any that are smoking hot.

What is the chimney's favorite soda?

Roof beer.

Do chimneys work hard?

Their work is exhausting.

Do chimneys complain?

Yeah, they're known for venting.

What does Santa say when he sees a pigeon's nest on the chimney?

He cries, "Fowl!"

How did Santa rise in the chimney?

He understands the "flew" part of the chimney.

Did the chimney have high goals?

It had grate expectations.

Are chimneys expensive
to install and maintain?

They are through the roof.

Can you trust
what a chimney says?

No; sometimes chimneys are full of hot air.

How are Santa and
a piece of bread alike?

If they are in your fireplace and you light a fire, they're toast.

Do warm fireplaces
inspire Santa to move quickly?

They keep the heat on him.

On Christmas Eve,
what did the watchdog say when asked where Santa was?

"Woof!"

CHRISTMAS CARDS

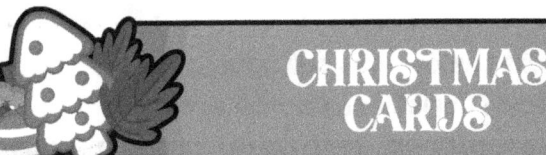

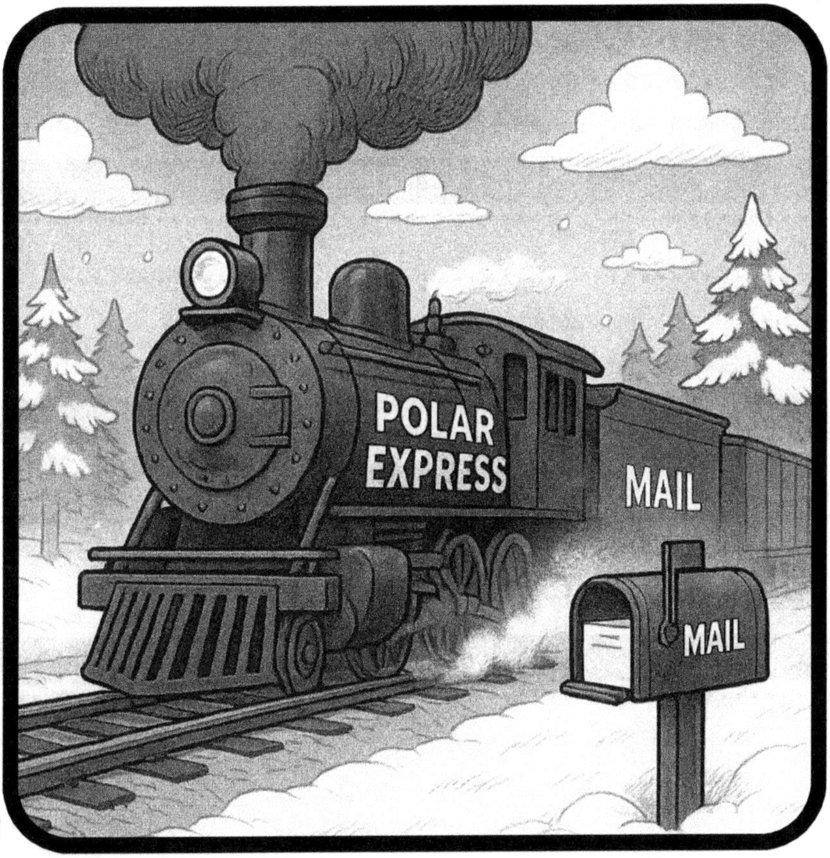

What type of mail
is used at the North Pole?

The Polar Express.

Why did the boy put salt and
pepper in each Christmas card he sent?

He wanted to send seasons' greetings.

What happened when the mail carrier pointed out the problem
that the envelope didn't have any routing information on it?

The man said he'd address it.

Are people happy when they have to
lick the envelopes of the Christmas cards they send?

No, it leaves a bad taste in their mouths.

What did the creative
Christmas card sender do?

Pushed the envelope.

CHRISTMAS CAROLS

What is the grape's favorite Christmas song?

"Tis the Season to be Jelly."

What is the llama's favorite Christmas chorus?

Fa-la-la, la-la-llama.

In addition to Christmas carols, what type of music do presents listen to?

Wrap.

What is the night-time golfer's favorite Christmas hymn?

"O, Holey Night."

What do you call facebook friends at Christmas?

Fa-a-la-ala-ollowers.

What spice is at its peak during the Christmas season?

Thyme: as the song says, "It's the most wonderful thyme of the year."

What material is used to make Christmas sweaters?

Fleece Navidad.

★ MERRY CHRISTMAS

Which Christmas carol do kings sing
when they want their army of men in armor to be still?

"Silent Knight."

23

CHRISTMAS COOKIES

What did one chocolate chip cookie predict
for the other cookie as Santa ate the first cookie?

"You're about to be desserted."

Why can't you tell cookies
any Christmas secrets?

They crumble under pressure.

What is the difference between the child who makes
the Christmas cookies and the jolly guy that eats
the Christmas cookies for refreshment on Christmas Eve?

One kneads cookies; the other needs cookies.

How is baking Christmas cookies
similar to playing poker?

The more chips you have, the better.

What is the sugar cookie's
favorite weather forecast?

It's not snow, silly; it's sprinkles!

How can you tell
if a Christmas cookie is rich?

It will have a lot of dough.

CHRISTMAS LIGHTS

 Why was the string of
Christmas lights nervous?

It was strung out.

Are Christmas lights social?

I'll say, if one goes out, they all do.

How should you informally
greet Christmas lights?

"Watts up?"

What did the lightbulb
say to its sad friend?

"Come on; lighten up."

Why do Christmas lights
know the best restaurants in town?

They are always going out.

CHRISTMAS ORNAMENTS

How is a
Christmas tree ornament like me?

The ornament is hooked on Christmas trees; I'm hooked on Christmas.

What did one ornament say to
encourage the other ornament?

"Hang in there."

What did the auto mechanic place on
his Christmas tree?

Hood ornaments.

Why was the ornament absent?

It was playing hooky elsewhere.

CHRISTMAS PRESENTS – CHOOSING GIFTS AND KEEPING SECRETS

Why didn't Santa
leave the blunt pencil as a gift?

He knew it was pointless.

Why can't you
tell a pig your Christmas secrets?

Pigs squeal.

Which fish can't
keep a Christmas secret?

The big-mouth bass.

What did the nun say when she found out
she was getting a new habit for Christmas?

"I'm getting nun thing for Christmas."

Why do shop clerks
who gift wrap make excellent spies?

They know how to keep things under wrap.

Why didn't anyone tell the owl
what was in the present to his sister?

He was always talon secrets.

CHRISTMAS PRESENTS - WRAPPING GIFTS

Why didn't the ribbon
have a more adventurous life?

It was tied down.

What does the ribbon do
when it gets tired?

It curls up.

Why did the gift call the ribbon attached
to it "my boyfriend"?

It was her beau.

Why did the ribbon feel nervous?

Its stomach was in knots.

What did the winning package
receive as a decoration?

A blue ribbon.

Why didn't the ribbon
come to the holiday party?

It was all tied up.

Why are gift-wrapped
arrows the perfect gift?

They come with a bow.

What did the bureaucrat wrap the present in?

Red tape.

Why did the door prize seeker dress in gift wrap?

He read that you must be present to win.

Why was the bow placed on the package?

Because it was knot decorated.

What kind of humor did the ribbon have?

Twisted.

What happened when the ribbon got angry?

It got bent out of shape.

What happened when the ribbon got questioned by the principal?

It became unraveled.

CHRISTMAS SPIRIT

Why did the girl yell, "One, two, three, four; it's Christmas time once more?"

She wanted to share holiday cheer.

What do you call the rising ocean level on December 25?

Yule tide.

Why do some people believe every day is Christmas?

Because it's present day.

What did Sherlock Holmes say
upon seeing the Christmas stocking?

"The holiday season is afoot."

How long is a typical Christmas stocking?

A foot. (That's 30.48 centimeters, just in case you're wondering.)

Why was the stocking accused of loitering?

It was just hanging around.

Why did the boy put his name
on his sock with thread?

He was sew inclined.

What distinguishes Christmas stockings
from other holiday decorations?

They often have a sole in them.

What makes a great sock stuffer?

A foot.

What would you expect to be
at the end of a Christmas stocking?

Mistle toes.

Why is filling the stockings Santa's favorite part of delivering gifts?

Stockings are his sole favorite.

What's the difference between toy makers at Christmas and grocery clerks at Thanksgiving?

At Christmas, we have stocking stuffers; at Thanksgiving, we have stuffing stockers.

Why did the sock spy on Santa as he delivered presents?

It was a Christmas stalking.

How is a bad habit like placing your stocking on the mantle?

Both are hang-ups.

Why did the stocking go to the doctor?

He was concerned about his mantle health.

Why was the phone nailed to the fireplace?

Mother told Junior to hang it up.

Why did the boy consider his tattered socks to be religious?

He heard his mom call them holy.

Do Christmas stockings help set the holiday mood?

Socks definitely get us into step.

What did the stocking say to the fireplace?

"I like hanging around you."

CHRISTMAS TREE

Why didn't Santa Claus leave
any gifts for the Christmas tree?

It was a naughty pine.

How is a hairless man
similar to a Christmas tree?

The hairless man is bald, and the Christmas tree is balled.

How did the Christmas tree make friends?

It branched out.

What do you call
a Christmas tree's journal?

A log.

What did one branch of
the Christmas tree say to the other?

"We need to stick together."

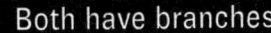

Why did the girl speak to a travel agent
about what was under her Christmas tree?

She wanted to arrange a package tour.

How are Christmas trees and banks alike?

Both have branches.

How did the Christmas tree
enhance the room?

It spruced it up.

What happened when the sentimental
Christmas tree got Santa-mental?

He got sappy.

What did the Christmas tree tell its adopted family
as it chopped him down to take him home?

"I'm falling for you."

What do you yell on a cold night
when felling a Christmas tree?

"Timb – br-br-br-br-brrrrrrr!"

Why did the famous actress sit on top of
the Christmas tree at the boy's request?

The boy wanted a star on top of his tree.

Did the Christmas tree have fun?

It had a ball.

What made the Christmas tree a haunted tree?

The presence underneath it.

What did the Christmas tree say to the candy cane?

Want to hang with me?

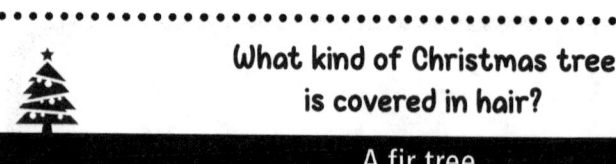

What kind of Christmas tree
is covered in hair?

A fir tree.

Why did the girl take her
Christmas tree to the barber?

It needed trimming.

Why can't you borrow money from elves?

They're always short.

Are there evolutionary reasons
why elves' ears are shaped as they are?

There are good points.

What do you call a competition between two elves to see
who can load the most presents for shipping?

A boxing match.

Why do elves that sing
get the most attention?

They are note-worthy.

What kind of elf gives up
his seat on the shelf?

A shelfless one.

Why didn't the elf get any praise
for doing a good job?

He was overlooked.

What kind of pictures do Santa's elves
like to take with their cell phones?

Elf-ies.

GINGERBREAD MEN

Why did the Gingerbread Man
go to the hospital?

He was feeling crumby.

Why did the Gingerbread Man go to
the Home Goods store when he remodeled his bedroom?

He needed a cookie sheet.

Why did Santa hire
the Gingerbread Man as a bodyguard?

He was one tough cookie.

NORTH POLE LIFE

Why is reaching the North Pole considered the greatest achievement one can have?

Because everything goes south from there.

What is the name of the school for nurses that is located at the North Pole?

Icy U.

How do they give birthday greetings at the North Pole?

Happy Brr-day.

Why is everybody at the North Pole so happy?

When you're at the North Pole, you're on top of the world.

Where do people at the North Pole keep their money?

In a snowbank.

Why don't people use the North Pole Bank?

All its assets are frozen.

What do you call a robin
that is at the North Pole?

A brrrrrrr-ird.

What did the comedian title
his Christmas special broadcast live from the North Pole?

Yule Laugh.

SANTA CLAUS AND MRS. CLAUS

What does Santa pay his bills with?

Cold hard cash.

Where does Santa like to swim?

The North Pool.

Why does Santa like get-to-know-you games?

He likes to break the ice.

Where does Santa go to vote?

The North Poll.

Can you believe Santa likes Chocolate milk, white milk, and even banana milk?

How dairy!

Why does Santa drink milk?

It's udderly refreshing.

Should Santa drink a big glass o eggnog before supper?

I think we all agree that it would be a pour decision.

How is Santa like a baseball umpire when he eats milk and cookies?

Both stand behind the plate.

Why were Santa's computers hacked so easily?

Santa accepts all cookies.

What jolly character brings presents to crows at Christmas?

Santa Caws.

What did Santa say after being hit with a snowball?

"That was cold."

Where does Santa go to get his hair cut
at the frigid North Pole?

The brr-brr shop.

Is it true that Santa has a maximum number of gifts
he will bring any one person?

Everyone knows Santa has a cap.

What does Santa say
when something goes wrong?

"No-No-No."

I wanted to help Santa choose my gifts,
so I wrote down ideas to share.

It was the list I could do.

What happened
when Santa grew out his fingernails?

He became Santa Claws.

Why does Santa tend to
give gifts in groups?

He likes package deals.

What do you call Santa
without a GPS?

A lost Claus.

From what does Santa
like to drink his root beer?

A Frosty mug.

**What's the difference between
Santa and a pirate?**

Santa says, "Ho-ho-ho," and a pirate says, "Yo-ho-ho."

Who goes "oh, oh, oh?"

Santa Claus walking backward.

What was Santa's nickname after he cut himself with his razor?

St. Nick.

Why is Santa so good with dogs?

Because he constantly asks them, "Who's a good boy?"

SANTA'S NAUGHTY-AND-NICE LIST

How did the baby describe
his behavior for the year?

"Goo-goo-good!"

Did Santa proclaim the ribbon
to be well-behaved?

No, he said it was knotty.

Why did the rope not get
any Christmas presents from Santa?

Santa knew it was knotty.

Why did the boy untie his shoes?

He didn't want them on Santa's knotty list.

What did the naughty girl
say to her mother at bedtime?

"Time for me to go naughty night, Mom."

SANTA'S SLEIGH AND REINDEER

Which animal is the scariest
at the North Pole?

The cari-boo.

Why did Santa take a duck
with him in his sleigh on Christmas Eve?

He had to get down from the sleigh many times.

What did Santa tell Rudolph
when Rudolph wanted to become an elf?

"Rudolph, be a dear."

Did you hear about the knight who hunted dragons
during the day and rode with Santa at night?

He slayed during the day, and he sleighed during the night.

Why couldn't the boy
name Santa's reindeer?

Santa had already named them.

**How are Santa's reindeer similar
to baseball players?**

Both are stopped by rein.

 **Why was Santa happy
when Rudolph got to be the lead reindeer?**

Rudolph was a deer friend.

SANTA'S WORKSHOP

Why can't elves disclose
how Santa makes spinning toys?

It's a top secret.

Why did Santa put
a "Help Wanted" sign on his workshop?

He was short staffed.

What did Santa say to the pokey elves
when he wanted to go home for the day?

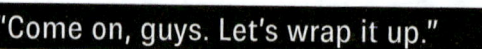

"Come on, guys. Let's wrap it up."

When Santa calls roll at the North Pole workshop,
how do the elves answer?

"Present."

What did Santa say to the elf
who made the perfectly constructed wooden birdhouse?

"You nailed it!"

How do the elves stay focused on making toys
and not daydreaming about the future?

They are present-minded.

SNOW AND WINTER WEATHER

What can you say about a snowstorm
that arrives exactly as the meteorologist predicted?

"It was white on time."

How excited were people to learn that it
was going to snow on Christmas Eve?

They were snow excited.

What do you call the news report
that says it's snowing?

Flake news!

What did Mom yell in reply after Junior
said winter precipitation was falling?

"Tell me it ain't snow!"

Does snow travel fast?

No, it travels in snow-motion.

Why did the detective enjoy winter?

He liked working cold cases.

What did the police officer
order the precipitation to do?

"Freeze!"

Is cold weather fun?

Only to a certain degree.

Did you hear about the man who loaned his coat to his wife on a negative ten-degree day?

Shivery isn't dead.

Is snow a winner?

Even if it's not, it gets a precipitation trophy.

What happens if Jack frost nips you on the neck?

You have Frost bite.

Where did the road-grader leave the snow that it scraped off the street?

In a snow parking zone.

Have you ever tried using a discount coupon to get snow off a car window?

With a coupon, you can get a small percentage off.

Why did the girl stand in front of
her class holding snow?

It was Snow and Tell Day.

What should you do on a cold winter's day to relax
if you should get cold outside?

Just chill.

What did the snowflake say
after it dropped a hint about the present?

"Do you get my drift?"

What kind of snow owns a car?

A driving snow.

How is skiing like
being naughty "just once"?

You're on a slippery slope.

Snow chills our fingers;
what does it make warm?

Hearts.

What kind of bedding do
polar bears prefer?

Sheets of ice and blankets of snow.

Why did the boy leave his joke book
in the cold outdoors?

He wanted to read some cool jokes.

Why did the nervous boy wear boots
for his presentation?

He didn't want to get cold feet.

How did the ski trip go?

Downhill.

What was the supermodel's
favorite type of snow?

Powder.

Why do you have to be careful
walking in heavy, powdery snow?

Because with great powder comes great responsibility.

How did the snow globe feel
after being dropped?

A bit shaken up.

How are a cold winter day
and a horror film alike?

Both are chilling.

Did Santa survive his trip around the world last year
despite the cold temperatures?

Brrrr-ly.

What encouragement
did one icicle give to the other?

"Hang in there."

Why are many people fascinated by people
who imitate Jack Frost?

Most make a good Frost impression.

What happens if an icicle falls on your head?

You'll get knocked out cold.

Why did the psychic like winter?

She liked doing cold readings.

Do you know what's really cool?

Winter.

Why did the kidney beans put on jackets?

They didn't want to become chili.

Why did the snowman
turn down a job offer?

Because he heard it was a flake-y position!

What did Mrs. Claus say when Santa asked,
"Have you heard today's weather forecast?"

"I looked outside and saw rain, dear."

When do meteorologists communicate the best?

When predicting a snowstorm, lots of people get the drift.

What is common headwear
for mountains in the winter?

Ice caps.

what do you get when you
cross a snowman and a dog?

Frostbite.

SNOWMEN AND SNOWWOMEN

Where do snow people dance?

Snowballs.

Why is it hard to be friends with a snowman?

He never warms up to you.

What kind of look did the snowman give when he got angry?

An icy stare.

How is a snowman like the ocean?

Both are bodies of water.

Why do snowmen try to avoid getting angry?

Meltdowns are not good for their health.

How can you tell rich snowmen
from poor snowmen?

The rich snowmen have a one-carrot nose.

 Are snowmen scatterbrained,
unreliable, and forgetful?

Yes, they are a bit flakey.

Why was the snowman arrested?

He had sticky fingers.

What prize did the snowman
win in the contest?

Best in snow.

What is the snowman's favorite
breakfast cereal?

He likes both Ice Crispies and Frosted Flakes.

Who is the most hip of all of
the Christmas characters?

Frosty the Snowman is certainly the coolest.

What is the snowman's
favorite part of the cupcake?

The icing.

What do you say to calm
an angry snowman?

"Chill."

What position did the snowman play on the baseball team?

Frost base.

Where did the snowman have to go to find his scarf?

The frost-and-found box.

How does a snowman say, "Good day"?

"Have an ice day."

What did the angry snowman
say to the chunks of coal that were teasing him?

"Get out of my face!"

How are men
who work out a lot like Yeti?

Men who work out are abdominal showmen,
and the Yeti is the Abominable Snowman.

WREATHS, HOLLY, AND MISTLETOE

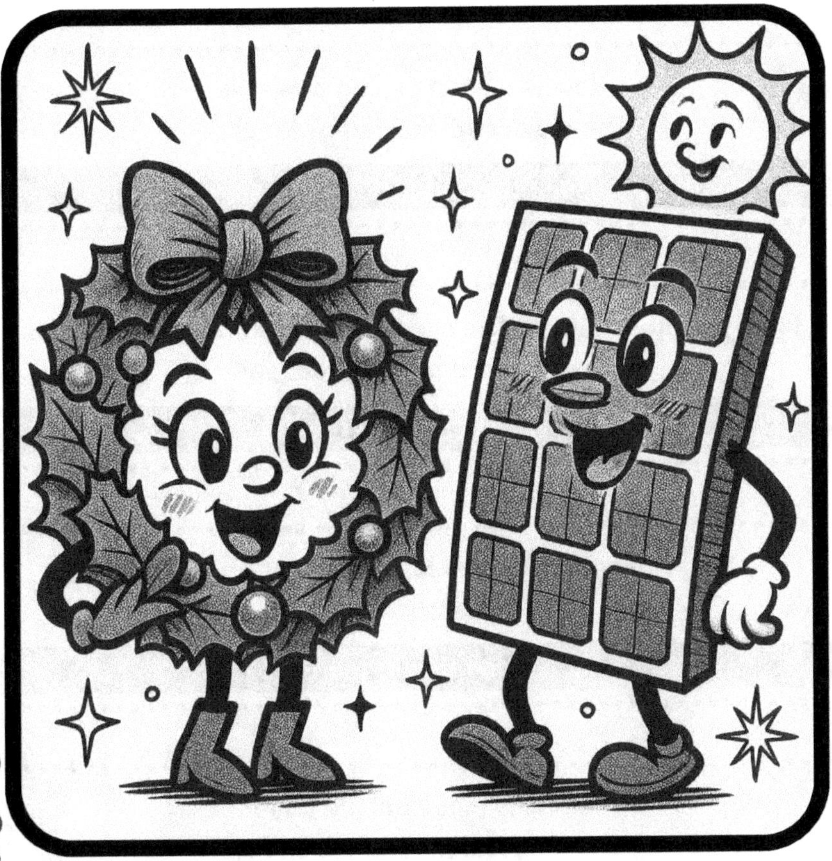

How are a Christmas wreath and solar power alike?

Both give a home green energy.

Why are wreaths round?

To ring in the Christmas season.

How is a Jeep pulling a missile
like a piece of holiday greenery?

One is a missile-tow, and the other is a mistletoe.

To be punny, what did the clownfish keep on his front door
during the holiday season?

A coral reef.

What animal hops and is very dangerous around
Christmastime?

The missile toad.

What is most unique about
the hospital at the North Pole?

The holly in the I.V.

Why are so many people enchanted
with holly this time of year?

It's the holly daze.

GIFT TWO:
HO-HO-HO-ING

Ho ho ho! That's my famous laugh—big, warm, and full of Christmas cheer. It's how everyone knows Santa has arrived. People say I'm a jolly fellow, and I suppose they're right. After all, laughter is part of the job description when you deliver joy to the whole world in one night.

But did you know "Ho Ho Ho" isn't just a sound? It's a feeling. It's the sparkle of happiness that fills a room when people share a good laugh. It's the echo of joy that bounces off the walls of my workshop when the elves hear a funny story. It's what keeps the Christmas spirit alive all year long.

And here's a little secret. You can be Ho Ho Ho-larious too. You don't need a red suit or flying reindeer. All you need is a happy heart and a good sense of humor. Try giving your best Ho Ho Ho the next time something funny happens. It works like magic. Even the grumpiest elf can't help but smile when they hear it.

Inside this chapter, you'll find jokes that capture that very spirit of laughter—playful, clever, and full of good cheer. They're the kind that make your cheeks ache from smiling and your belly shake like a bowl full of jelly.

So go ahead and spread the joy. Share a laugh, tell a joke, and keep that Ho Ho Ho spirit shining bright. The world can always use a little more laughter, especially the kind that jingles.

Have you ever heard Santa tell a joke?

He is Ho-Ho-Ho-larious.

Where does Santa sleep on vacation?

A Ho-Ho-Hotel.

What does Santa do in his garden?

Ho-Ho-Hoe.

Where does Santa like to relax
at the end of the day?

Ho-Ho-Home.

What does Santa have that
makes him optimistic?

Ho-Ho-Hope.

Why did Santa get his socks patched?

They were Ho-Ho-Holey.

What does Santa use to
get water to the reindeer?

A Ho-Ho-Hose.

What does Santa say
when he wants you to stop?

"Ho-Ho-Hold it!"

How does Santa cheer?

"Ho-Ho-Hooray!"

What does Santa call the plot of pretending
to be good but not really being good?

"A Ho-Ho-Hoax."

What kind of stockings
does Mrs. Claus wear?

Ho-Ho-Hose.

What does Santa say
when he wants the elves to be serious?

"Quit Ho-Ho-Ho-rsing around."

What kind of scary films
does Santa sometimes watch?

Ho-Ho-Horror.

What is Santa's favorite sandwich?

The Ho-Ho-Hoagie.

What does Santa want to hit
with the bases loaded in a baseball game?

A Ho-Ho-Homerun!

What does Santa read to see
what astrologists predict for him?

His Ho-Ho-Horoscope.

How does Santa
describe the place of worship?

"Ho-Ho-Holy."

What does the street in front of
Santa's house have?

Ho-Ho-Holes.

How much of the pie did Santa eat?

The Ho-Ho-Whole thing.

What does Santa say
when he is bored?

"Ho-Ho-Ho-Hum."

How did Santa describe his voice
after Ho-Ho-Ho-ing all day?

"I'm Ho-Ho-Ho-rse."

What instrument does Santa play?

The Ho-Ho-Horn.

What does Santa call to Mrs. Claus
when he returns from delivering gifts worldwide?

"I'm Ho-Ho-Home."

What does Santa celebrate at
Christmas, Easter, and Halloween?

A Ho-Ho-Holiday.

GIFT THREE:
KNOCK-KNOCK JOKES

Ho ho ho! You've made it all the way to your third gift—now that's what I call commitment to Christmas cheer. This one is especially close to my heart, because it celebrates the kind of laughter that comes right to your door.

Christmas is the busiest travel season of the year. Families pack up sleighs, trains, and cars to visit loved ones near and far, and all that coming and going means plenty of knocks at the door. That's why this next set of jokes fits the season perfectly—they're all about knocking!

Believe it or not, there's a whole style of humor built around that simple sound: knock, knock. It's one of the oldest joke formats in the book, and it always brings a smile because everyone can join in. One person knocks, the other answers, and before you know it, everyone's laughing.

So, think of these as tiny visitors tapping at your imagination, each one bringing a little bundle of humor from the North Pole. Inside you'll find Christmas-themed knock-knock jokes that will have elves chuckling, reindeer snickering, and snowmen shaking with laughter.

Open the door, welcome the jokes inside, and let the laughter fill your home.

Knock-Knock.
Who's there?
Chillin'
Chillin', who?
Chillin' like you and I get to stay up later than our younger siblings.

Knock-Knock.
Who's there?
Advent.
Advent, who?
Advent to the store to buy a present.

Knock-Knock.
Who's there?
Wrap City.
Wrap City, who?
Wrap City and other exciting feelings find me at Christmas time.

Knock-Knock.
Who's there?
Who Who.
Who Who, who?
That's a pretty weak Santa impression that you have there.

Knock-Knock.
Who's there?
Starbucks.
Starbucks, who?
Starbucks for Santa are Rudolph and Blitzen.

Knock-Knock.
Who's there?
Mel Ting.
Mel Ting, who?
Mel Ting snow always makes me sad, especially if my snowman disappears.

Knock-Knock.
Who's there?
Myrrh.
Myrrh, who?
Myrrh jokes would be fine with me.

Knock-Knock.
Who's there?
Fir.
Fir, who?
Fir sure going to have a great Christmas this year.

Knock-Knock.
Who's there?
Thawed Out.
Thawed Out, who?
Thawed Out my Christmas plans; have you thought out yours?

Knock-Knock.
Who's there?
Yule Log.
Yule Log, who?
Yule Log the door after letting me in, won't you?

Knock-Knock.
Who's there?
Icey.
Icey, who?
Icey what you did there.

Knock-Knock.
Who's there?
Noel.
Noel, who?
No elephants passed this point.

Knock-Knock.
Who's there?
Alice.
Alice, who?
Alice (a list) of all the good boys and girls is what Santa keeps.

Knock-Knock.
Who's there?
Mai Ling.
Mail Ling, who?
Mailing or e-mailing Santa your wish list is okay this year.

Knock-Knock.
Who's there?
Holly.
Holly who?
Holly days like Hanukkah, Kawunza, New Year's Day, and Christmas are coming.

Knock-Knock.
Who's there?
Noel.
Noel, who?
No "L" means the alphabet is incomplete.

Knock-Knock.
Who's there?
Harriett.
Harriett, who?
Harriett up; I want Christmas to be here tomorrow.

Knock-Knock.
Who's there?
Holly.
Holly, who?
Holly-lelujah, on Christmas, many people celebrate Jesus's birthday.

Knock-Knock.
Who's there?
Peppermint.
Peppermint, who?
Peppermint is for some foods; salt is meant for others.

Knock-Knock.
Who's there?
Naughty.
Naughty, who?
Naughty yule logs don't burn very well.

Knock-Knock.
Who's there?
Snow Bored.
Snow Bored, who?
Snow Bored is one of my favorite things to ride in the snow; I also like my sled.

Knock-Knock.
Who's there?
Rudolph.
Rudolph, who?
Rudolph you not to open the door for me.

Knock-Knock.
Who's there?
Pole Ice.
Pole Ice, who?
Pole Ice are looking for the Grinch, who stole all the presents from Whoville.

Knock-Knock.
Who's there?
Snow.
Snow, who?
Snow need to cry if your snowman melts; there will be more snow on another day.

Knock-Knock.
Who's there?
Joey.
Joey, who?
Joey to the world; it's Christmas time!

Knock-Knock.
Who's there?
Soot.
Soot, who?
Soot of red with white trim and a red hat is what Santa will likely be wearing.

Knock-Knock.
Who's there?
Dachshund.
Dachshund, who?
Dachshund through the snow, in a one-horse open sleigh . . .

Knock-Knock.
Who's there?
New Dolls.
New Dolls, who?
New Dolls are good in both casseroles and spaghetti.

Knock-Knock.
Who's there?
Fir.
Fir, who?
Fir-get all your troubles and enjoy the Christmas spirit.

Knock-Knock.
Who's there?
Elf.
Elf, who?
Elf it snows, we will have a white Christmas.

Knock-Knock.
Who's there?
Naughty.
Naughty, who?
Naughty, not coffee; not soda – it's hot chocolate!

Knock-Knock.
Who's there?
Al B.
Al B., who?
Al B. counting the days until Christmas.

Knock-Knock.
Who's there?
Aretha Holly.
Aretha Holly, who?
Aretha Holly would look good on the front door.

Knock-Knock.
Who's there?
No L.
No L, who?
No L is a french word for Christmas.

Knock-Knock.
Who's there?
Carolyn.
Carolyn, who?
Carolyn and hot chocolate go together.

Knock-Knock.
Who's there?
Megan.
Megan, who?
Megan a list and checking it twice.

Knock-Knock.
Who's there?
Stan Ding.
Stan Ding, who?
Stan Ding in line to see Santa.

Knock-Knock.
Who's there?
Bow.
Bow, who.
Bow of cereal is what I had for breakfast today.

Knock-Knock.
Who's there?
Advent.
Advent, who?
Advent-ures await us this holiday season.

Knock-Knock.
Who's there?
Icy Yule.
Icy Yule, who?
Icy Yule be busy this holiday season.

Knock-Knock.
Who's there?
Naughty.
Naughty, who?
Naughty creature was stirring, not even a mouse.

Knock-Knock.
Who's there?
Elvis.
Elvis, who?
Elvis busy loading the sleigh; Santa is getting dressed - the big night is almost here!

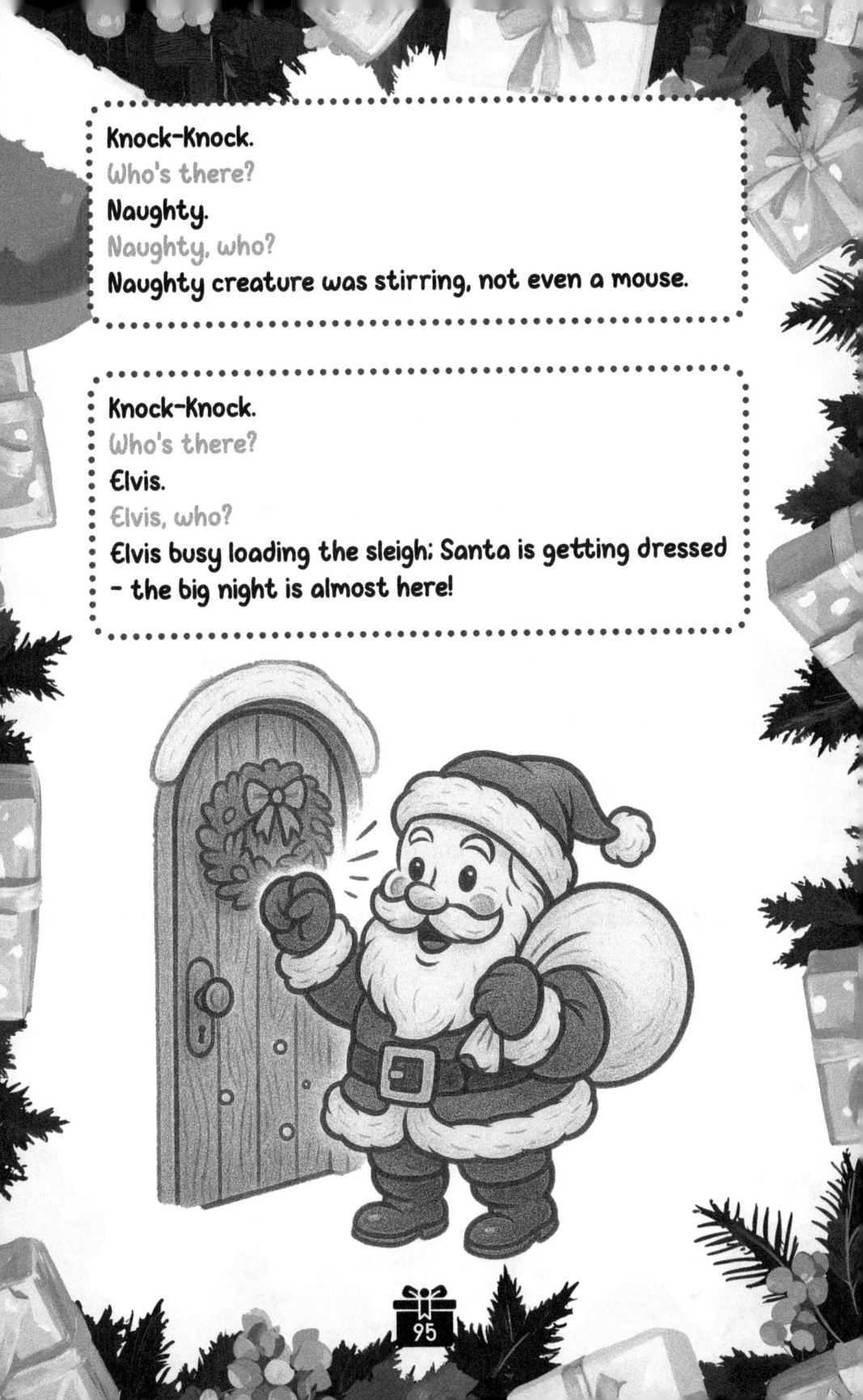

DID YOU ENJOY THE BOOK?

If you did, we are ecstatic. If not, please write your complaint to us and we will ensure we fix it.

If you're feeling generous, there is something important that you can help me with – tell other people that you enjoyed the book.

Ask a grown-up to write about it on Amazon. When they do, more people will find out about the book. It also lets Amazon know that we are making kids around the world laugh. Even a few words and ratings would go a long way.

If you have any ideas or jokes that you think are super funny, please let us know. We would love to hear from you. Our email address is -

riddleland@riddlelandforkids.com

ABOUT RIDDLELAND

Riddleland is a mum + dad run publishing company. We are passionate about creating fun and innovative books to help children develop their reading skills and fall in love with reading. If you have suggestions for us or want to work with us, shoot us an email at riddleland@riddlelandforkids.com
Our family's favorite quote:

"Creativity is an area in which younger people have a tremendous advantage since they have an endearing habit of always questioning past wisdom and authority."

~ Bill Hewlett